Cello Time Sprinters

Piano accompaniment book

Kathy and David Blackwell

T0088429

Contents

1.	Carnival jig	2
2.	Spic and span	3
4.	Stop—start	4
5.	River song	5
6.	Overture: A Baroque celebration	6
7.	Going fourth	8
8.	City streets	9
10.	Metro line	10
11.	Falling leaves	11
12.	Holiday in Havana	12
14.	Night shift	14
15.	Le Tambourin (Rameau)	14
17.	Beyond the horizon	16
18.	Sto me	17
20.	Andante (Elgar)	18
21.	Joker in the pack	19
23.	Comin' home	20
24.	Sprint finish	22
25.	In memory	23
26.	Some day	24
27.	Wild West	26
28.	Je pense à toi	28
29.	Russian wedding	30
30.	Two Songs from Dichterliebe (Schumann)	32
31.	Latin nights	34
32.	4th dimension	36
33.	Fifth Avenue	38

MUSIC DEPARTMENT

OXFORD
UNIVERSITY PRESS

1. Carnival jig

KB & DB

© Oxford University Press 2005 and 2014

Printed in Great Britain

OXFORD UNIVERSITY PRESS, MUSIC DEPARTMENT, GREAT CLARENDON STREET, OXFORD OX2 6DP

The Moral Rights of the Composers have been asserted. Photocopying this copyright material is ILLEGAL.

2. Spic and span

KB & DB

4. Stop—start

KB & DB

5. River song

KB & DB

6. Overture

A Baroque celebration

KB & DB

22
mp
f
dim.
mp
28
cresc.
cresc.
33
f
mp
cresc.
f
mp
cresc.
39
mf
cresc.
ff
poco rit.
mf
cresc.
ff

7. Going fourth

KB & DB

With thanks to Tom Morter for this idea.

8. City streets

KB & DB

10. Metro line

KB & DB

11. Falling leaves

KB & DB

12. Holiday in Havana

KB & DB

17
mf
21
mp
25
p
p
29
f
ff
f
ff

14. Night shift

KB & DB

15. Le Tambourin

J. Ph. Rameau (1683–1764)
(adapted)

A tambourin was a lively 18th-century French dance, often accompanied by pipe and tabor.

(8)
f
f
13
p
17
cresc.
mp
f
p
cresc.
mp
21
f

17. Beyond the horizon

KB & DB

18. Sto me

Bulgarian trad.

With energy

20. Andante

Edward Elgar (1857–1934)

21. Joker in the pack

KB & DB

23. Comin' home

KB & DB

24
pizz.
mf
30
arco
(mf)
36
cresc.
f
ff
cresc.
f
ff
41
dim.
mf
rall.
pizz.
dim.
mf

24. Sprint finish

KB & DB

25. In memory

(*for Eileen*)

KB & DB

26. Some day

KB & DB

21
mf
26
31
cresc.
cresc.
37
mp
mp
Slower
42
p
p
pp

27. Wild West

KB & DB

16
cresc.
f
cresc.
f
20
24
28
ff
ff

28. Je pense à toi

(*for Clare*)

KB & DB

28
cresc.
cresc.
retenu
très retenu
1er mouvt
35
f
p
f
pp doucement
41
mp
cresc.
mp cresc.
48
mf cresc.
f
1.
2.
mf
f
mf

29. Russian wedding

31
Slower
p
mf
39
a tempo
8va
mp
46
f
cresc.
54
ff

30. Two Songs from Dichterliebe

1. The lovely month of May

Robert Schumann (1810–56)
(adapted)

The repeat is written out in the cello part.

2. The rose and the lily

31. Latin nights

Tango

KB & DB

Con fuoco

The last repeat is written out in the cello part.

32. 4th dimension

KB & DB

9
ff
ff
11
13
f
mf
mf
15
mp
rall.
Slow
p
dim.
mp
p

33. Fifth Avenue

(*for lain*)

18
23
(1)
mp
cresc.
mp
27
cresc.
f
1.
cresc.
f
1.
31
mp
2.
ff
mp
f
2.
ff